Amazing Colouring Book

Discovering GOD together

Little Worship Company Amazing Me (Series 1) Colouring Book
© The Little Worship Company Ltd 2020
Cover designed by Rachael Fisher • With thanks to Lee Bruce, Sarah Joy, Rachael Fisher, Jo Sunderland and Jolie Greenwood.
Scripture quotations marked "NIV" are taken from The Holy Bible, New International Version® Anglicized, NIV®.
Copyright © 1979, 1984, 2011 by Biblica, Inc.®. Used by permission. All rights reserved worldwide.
Scripture quotations marked "LWC" are original translations by The Little Worship Company (in consultation with Wycliffe Bible Translators).
ISBN: 978-1-9160820-6-9

Introduction

At **Little Worship Company**, our heart is to inspire and delight children with a knowledge of God, and to support them as they begin to take their first steps of faith. We also want to help parents as they walk with their children on this wonderful journey. Our range of beautifully crafted, Biblically-based resources have been designed with the whole family in mind. So that all of God's children, little ones and bigger ones, can discover more of God and His incredible love together.

The Bible verses featured in this colouring book are all taken from **Little Worship Company DVD Series 1**, helping children learn more about the God who made them, loves them and has created an amazing world for them to live in.

As you and your child enjoy this colouring book, talk about the pictures and the Bible verses, share them with friends and family. **The Big Little Devotional Guide** is a great way to develop your child's understanding further and help start your family on a journey to discover more of God together.

All our products are available to buy on our website.

www.littleworshipcompany.com

Discovering GOD together